An Atlas of Rural Settlement in England

An Atlas of Rural Settlement in England

Brian K Roberts and Stuart Wrathmell

ENGLISH HERITAGE

2000

Copyright © English Heritage

First published 2000 by
English Heritage, 23 Savile Row
London W1S 2ET

Printed by Snoeck-Ducaju & Zoon, Ghent

ISBN 1 85074 770 9
Product code XC 20040

A CIP catalogue record for this book is available from the British Library

Design by English Heritage and Pauline Hull Design
Edited and brought to press by Karen Dorn and Andrew McLaren, Publications, English Heritage
Print production by Richard Jones, Publications, English Heritage

CONTENTS

FIGURES

ACKNOWLEDGEMENTS

The idea and maps embodied in this Atlas were stimulated by work we undertook at the request of David Stocker. There can be no doubt that his support and mentoring on behalf of English Heritage have been fundamental to the broader pattern of enquiry which has emerged as we continue to explore the many research themes deriving from the basic study. When David was unavailable, Graham Fairclough stepped in to sustain and encourage our efforts. We are grateful to both, and to English Heritage, for the support given to this project.

In many ways the maps are a joint effort involving Brian K Roberts and the Cartographic Team in the Department of Geography, University of Durham: Steven Allan drew the base maps; Arthur Corner undertook the daunting task of creating the terrain map – conceived in black and white because of the uncertainties of eventually achieving colour printing – and oversaw the training of Chris Orton. However, it was Chris who finally imposed a professional style upon Brian K Roberts' 'rough-cut' maps, undertaking much revision, while in the latter stages the ready advice and support of David Hume were always present.

Rosalyn ('Roz') Leighton created the first version of the terrain map: circumstances were such that she often worked without close supervision, yet subsequent reassessment has invariably vindicated her judgements. To her as well fell much routine assembly of other material: her sustained support was valued.

All the sources from which we have drawn material to integrate into the versions of the maps presented here are specifically acknowledged on each map, but particular thanks are due to the Ordnance Survey for allowing the use of the 1922 map as a base, and the estate of Harry Margary for the use of three sample map sections.

Finally, we must thank Karen Dorn, Managing Editor of English Heritage Publications, for her editorial advice.

AUTHORS' PREFACE

The idea for an atlas of rural settlement originated some six years ago, at a time when the authors were assisting English Heritage in the selection of medieval settlement remains for statutory protection. Such protection is available to sites which can be demonstrated to be of national importance on the basis of criteria such as the quality of site preservation, the quality of relevant historical documentation and the nature of formal characteristics. Until 1994 these criteria did not, however, overtly take account of the marked regional variations in rural settlement, and a decision was taken to treat regional diversity in rural settlement as itself a matter of national importance. This in turn necessitated the mapping which is presented in this Atlas. It was possible to assemble a full national picture in under two years of work using the Old Series Ordnance Survey one inch to one mile maps from the early and middle decades of the nineteenth century, published by Harry Margary, giving coverage for a period spanning less than seventy years. This framework possesses ancient roots, and is now used to inform the selection process.

The mapping and characterisations which appear in this Atlas should be seen, therefore, not as definitive statements on regional diversity, but rather, as an initial attempt to provide an alternative perspective on historic regional variation. Regional studies are often packaged in terms of historic counties or current administrative units: this is perhaps inevitable because these units structure some of the principal components of the historical and archaeological record. Yet a glance at the rural settlement mapping of Warwickshire, for instance, in the heart of England, makes clear the enormous diversity of settlement and land-use which can be found in this ancient administrative county; it indicates how, in their experience of social and economic conditions, the people of the south-eastern parts of the county would have had far less in common with their neighbours in the county's north-western portions than with those who inhabited adjacent counties to the east. Warwickshire is, perhaps, the best-known case of such marked internal contrasts, and is often cited, but no English county ever possessed complete uniformity of historic settlement pattern or agrarian structure. Our aim in publishing the settlement and terrain maps and the regional models is to address such issues at a national scale, the essential context for studies at other scales, and to encourage, inform and frame debate at a time when regional diversity and identity are again becoming much more significant themes generally in our lives.

FOREWORD

'What is the use of a book', thought Alice, 'without pictures or conversation?'

Alice in Wonderland, Chapter 1

Although grappling with archaeological and geographical theory, this Atlas was initially conceived to serve a very practical purpose: to provide English Heritage's *Monuments Protection Programme* with a national framework for evaluating medieval settlement sites (English Heritage 1996). Typically MPP reviews take a monument type (round barrows for example) at a national level, but it had become clear that this system was unsatisfactory for identifying and analysing post-Roman settlement remains. The Medieval Settlement Research Group pointed out that the problem lay with an outdated terminology of post-Roman settlement studies, based on concepts of desertion (as in the terms 'Deserted', 'Shrunken' and 'Shifted' Medieval Village). The academic debate had moved on to identify settlements according to the character of their nucleation rather than the extent to which they were deserted. Consequently, in 1994 English Heritage asked Dr Stuart Wrathmell to produce two new 'monument class descriptions' (MCDs) for nucleated and dispersed settlement and then, using the new MCDs, to review data-sets maintained by local government Sites and Monuments Records in order to select settlement sites of all types that might be candidates for statutory protection. Basing his review on twenty-five years' work on the mapping of settlements by Professor Brian K Roberts, Wrathmell showed how post-Roman settlement in England displays marked patterning. In some areas the landscape contains only nucleated settlements, while in others there is only a thin scattering of dispersed settlement types. Many areas, however, have distinctively different combinations of both nucleated and dispersed settlement types. The archaeological challenge now was to attempt a systematic 'characterisation' of the variety of settlement forms in each area of England.

The potential of such a characterisation of settlement diversity in England would have an impact on many areas of archaeological research as well as on the management of the archaeological resource. Roberts and Wrathmell proposed a new synthesis of many huge data-sets of settlements to generate meaningful maps of settlement types at a national scale. If they could do this satisfactorily, they argued, then they could establish a framework that would not only permit multifarious types of settlements to be understood within a national context but would also provide a theoretical construct against which post-Roman archaeology could be re-assessed. This aim was sufficiently interesting, both as a theoretical exercise and as a practical tool, that English Heritage was pleased to commission the research and publication of this Atlas.

Over the past decade or two the archaeological profession has been engaged in major syntheses of existing data, highlighting their full potential and posing questions for future research (Olivier, forthcoming). For most categories of archaeology, these syntheses have been carried out on a regional level to search for patterns not apparent at the level of the single site. There comes a point, however, when data-sets are too large, or categorisation too complex, to permit this sort of analysis, and a higher level of synthesis is required. This level, located above that of the individual site or group of sites and often using mapping at a much higher scale, will smooth out local irregularities to create a larger picture. Any national synthesis of post-Roman settlement data would be carried out at this higher level, though its conclusions may appear to be contradicted by data from individual sites.

The character of a settlement can be defined by reference to a variety of variables: topographic location, date of establishment, plan form, field-system type, number and type of properties, location of churches, social hierarchy of inhabitants, and differences in their access to resources. For each settlement site there may be hundreds of variables and there are many tens of thousands of settlement sites in England. Previous approaches to the characterisation of settlement types have gathered data on such variables in increasing detail and have been based on the presumption that sufficient data would eventually reveal national patterns. Considering the total number of variables to be recorded and manipulated in order to define the 'character' of a settlement, however, it is clear that a national data-collection exercise, followed by research, is not a realistic project for our generation. Empirical methodologies of this type are no longer practical for MPP needs. Nevertheless, the fact that data gathering proceeds slowly does not mean that it is not worthwhile. Indeed this 'bottom-up' methodology has underpinned almost all important work undertaken in the field, and it will surely continue to represent an excellent investment of research funding. Nevertheless, MPP needed to explore a different *modus operandi* if we were to propose an effective characterisation of post-Roman settlement types.

The work contained in this Atlas represents a radical break with empirical research methodology. Using a variety of existing data-sets, Roberts and Wrathmell have mapped the patterning visible in them at a national scale, fully aware of the imperfections this approach inevitably contains. In contrast with the empirical 'bottom-up' methodology, we have thought of this work as 'top-down'. We are clear, however, that valuable though we have found the 'top-down' approach for our purposes, it is not a replacement for 'bottom-up' work; the two are complementary. Data gathering will continue to be essential, but it can considered within the intellectual framework provided by this Atlas. Conversely, as researchers in the field undertake more and more field work, and compare their results with the Atlas, the Atlas itself will change, details refined, and the time-depth and mobility of settlement area boundaries elucidated. Indeed the Atlas includes several maps of such 'bottom-up' distributions, produced independently, and sometimes of considerable age, that display striking concurrence with the major boundaries identified by the Atlas itself (for example, the distribution of deserted medieval villages and pagan Anglo-Saxon burials). These fascinating coincidences between the distribution of various monument types nationally and the fundamental structure of settlement in England, revealed for the first time by the Atlas, are explored in a companion volume due to be published shortly by English Heritage (Roberts and Wrathmell forthcoming).

This Atlas, then, is a first attempt to sketch out the broad patterns of post-Roman settlement in England. It stands squarely in the tradition of Sir Cyril Fox (1932), Sir Clifford Darby (1951) and Joan Thirsk (1987). Furthermore it appears at a time when 'national characterisations' are being developed by other conservation bodies (eg Countryside Commission 1996). Along with initiatives such as *Yesterday's World, Tomorrow's Landscape* (Fairclough *et al*, 2000), this Atlas represents English Heritage's contribution to these broader developments. Taken as a group they underpin more selective conservation designations, such as Scheduling, Listing and the declaration of Conservation Areas, that allow the historic environment to be considered and managed as a whole. The Atlas is potentially an important tool for all aspects of settlement studies; it proposes a new interpretation of previous work and points to new directions for future research. We hope that it will be used, as well as read, by archaeologists and historians alike.

David Stocker
Inspector of Ancient Monuments
English Heritage

1 Introduction

This Atlas is constructed around a set of maps which chronicle in close detail the patterns of rural settlement present in nineteenth-century England. These show the existence of distinctive patterns, presences and absences, concentrations and scatters, which together divide England into three broad provinces. We will argue that these represent deep structures which are directly linked to the distribution of cleared lands and wooded lands over a thousand years earlier.

These provinces also frame contexts in which can be studied the ingredients of medieval settlement landscapes: nucleated villages, dispersed farmsteads and industrial hamlets, moated sites and upland shielings, together with constituents of land-usage such as the arable strips of the townfields, the common pastures and marshlands and the woodlands. For this reason the provinces have proved to be useful in that part of the English Heritage Monuments Protection Programme dealing with medieval sites. However, creating maps of past landscapes is fraught with problems, and our underlying philosophy can be illustrated by turning to an example drawn from a very different context.

The anthropologist Hugh Brody, in his book *Maps and Dreams*, asked a group of the Beaver people, forest hunters of the Canadian sub-arctic, to mark their hunting territories on 1:250,000 topographic maps, using simple lines made with fibre-tipped pens. His comment upon the results captures some of the patterns of reasoning which are important when working with all maps:

> There are lines that again and again appear in the same places. There are whole circles that neatly sit on top of the other. Such coincidences suggest that everyone is telling the same lie or the same truth. Since each hunter did his own map, often without having seen anyone else's, there is no reason for thinking that there was a conspiracy to distort data. Correspondence constitutes reasonable evidence of truth ... The most important test, however, is the way each community's aggregated map fits alongside the others ... Moreover, there is an important correspondence between the results and the terrain ... [B]etween them the community areas cover most of the available ground; yet they do not impinge upon each other. These maps were drawn community by community. There was no collaboration between the mappers of the different reserves. The systematic pattern that emerges is a reflection of reality ...
>
> (Brody 1981, 175–6)

Maps need not be complicated, yet even the simplest can lead towards more complex lines of reasoning. Super-imposition, comparison, coincidence, correspondence and convergence are key words in the use of maps as research tools. These are the key ideas which underlie the creation of this Atlas. James Corner takes us more deeply into what lines and shapes in landscapes and on maps can mean:

> Measure is intrinsic to the design, habitation, and representation of land. It underlies the variety of ways land is traversed and negotiated; it enables the spacing, marking, delineation, and occupation of a given terrain; it reflects the values and judgements of the society that live upon the land. Whether for purposes of navigation, cultivation, protection, or security, measure is taken to orient a particular reality, guiding a society's relationship to the land qualitatively as well as quantatively. Measure, then, is as much a conceptual apparatus as it is a mode of representation, facilitating events while constructing a particular cultural world
>
> (Corner and MacLean 1996, 41)

This Atlas is one step in constructing an understanding of the cultural world of English rural settlement from Anglo-Saxon times to the mid-nineteenth century. Indeed, some of the measures represented on the following maps have resonances in even earlier settlement data.

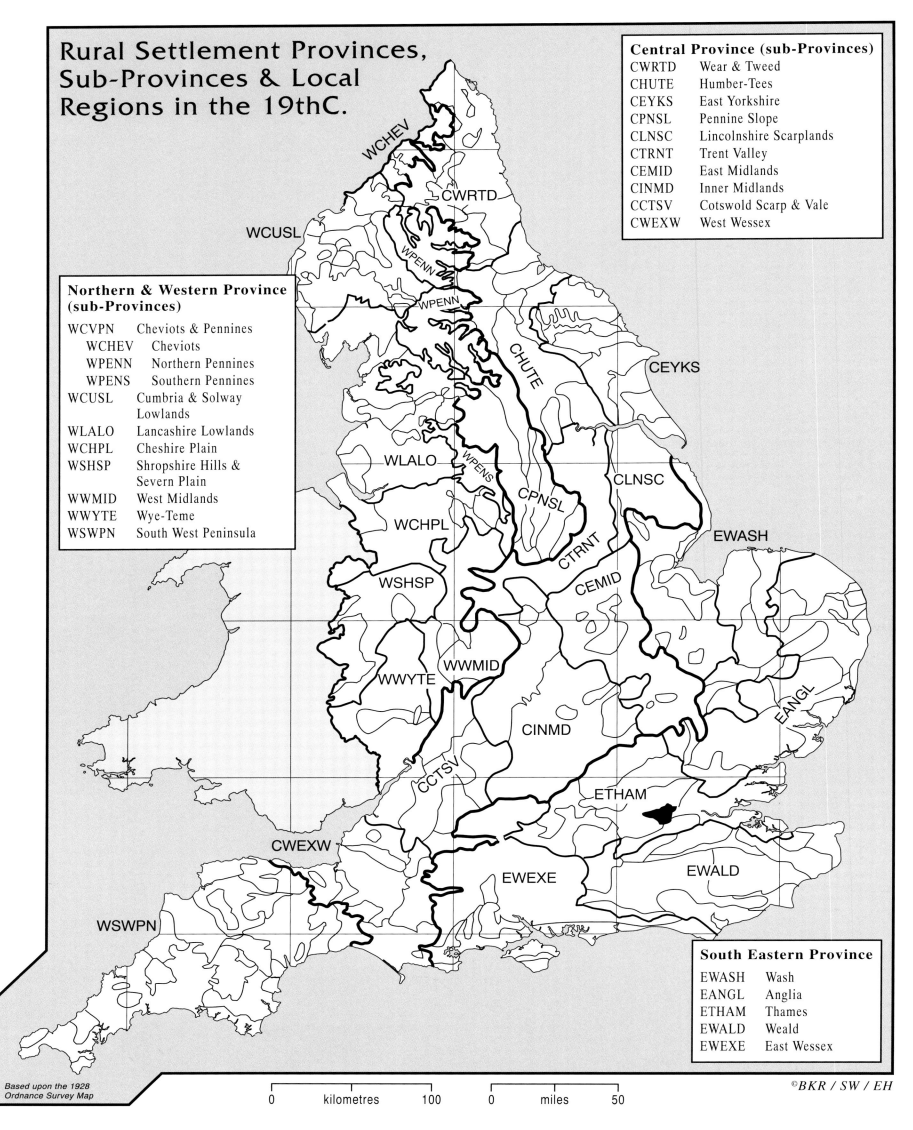

Rural Settlement Provinces, Sub-Provinces & Local Regions in the 19thC.

Central Province (sub-Provinces)

CWRTD	Wear & Tweed
CHUTE	Humber-Tees
CEYKS	East Yorkshire
CPNSL	Pennine Slope
CLNSC	Lincolnshire Scarplands
CTRNT	Trent Valley
CEMID	East Midlands
CINMD	Inner Midlands
CCTSV	Cotswold Scarp & Vale
CWEXW	West Wessex

Northern & Western Province (sub-Provinces)

WCVPN	Cheviots & Pennines
WCHEV	Cheviots
WPENN	Northern Pennines
WPENS	Southern Pennines
WCUSL	Cumbria & Solway Lowlands
WLALO	Lancashire Lowlands
WCHPL	Cheshire Plain
WSHSP	Shropshire Hills & Severn Plain
WWMID	West Midlands
WWYTE	Wye-Teme
WSWPN	South West Peninsula

South Eastern Province

EWASH	Wash
EANGL	Anglia
ETHAM	Thames
EWALD	Weald
EWEXE	East Wessex

Based upon the 1928 Ordnance Survey Map

0 kilometres 100   0 miles 50

©BKR / SW / EH

Figure 1

2 Background, aims and theory

Medieval rural settlement in England is marked by great diversity in form, size and type. The protection of archaeological remains needs to take these regional differences into account. To do this England has been divided into three broad Provinces on the basis of each area's distinctive mixture of nucleated and dispersed settlements: these can be further divided into sub-provinces and local regions. All of these possess regional characteristics which have gradually evolved during the past 1500 or more years.

English Heritage's Monuments Protection Programme: Standard paragraph for medieval rural settlement sites

At the core of this Atlas are two sets of maps: one presenting variations in the forms and densities of English rural settlement in the mid-nineteenth century, the other presenting variations in terrain. They constitute a starting point for exploring settlement variations in earlier centuries – accepting that some elements of the mid-nineteenth century pattern were then of recent origin, whilst others were undoubtedly centuries, if not millennia, old. This study has been built upon the earlier cartographic analyses of one of the authors, though in some ways its roots can be traced back to William Harrison's recognition, in the sixteenth century, of two Englands: one marked by villages and large arable townfields, the other represented by dispersed settlements in wood-pasture landscapes (Homans 1960, 21). As work has progressed, it has drawn into its ambit other national studies, notably those of Sir Clifford Darby on Domesday data, and of Oliver Rackham on the history of the English countryside. It has led to the definition of a hierarchy of regions with distinctive mixtures of settlement and land-use forms, and these have provided the basis for regional characterisation.

Background to the mapping project

No research project is ever conceived as a fully developed entity; initial ideas require a period of maturation before they can be expected to achieve serious consideration by the wider community. From the original idea of mapping rural settlement diversity, this present project could have followed many trajectories: for example, the chosen scale and methodology might have been closer to that followed by the Leverhulme funded project to map medieval settlement in four Midland counties (Lewis *et al* 1997). The selection of what is, fundamentally, a very different approach to often similar data was conditioned in several respects by the circumstances in which the project was initiated, and which guided its early development. A brief review of its initial content and guiding influences is, therefore, an appropriate place to start.

For practical purposes the starting point may be taken to be an invitation, in 1992, by English Heritage's Monuments Protection Programme to review the existing Monument Class Descriptions (MCDs) which had been developed in the mid-1980s for medieval settlement sites.

The aim of the MCDs was to provide a rational basis for assessing the 'national importance' of each recorded settlement site – and thereby for determining which sites warranted scheduling as Ancient Monuments. These preliminary MCDs had been largely shaped by the general thrust of medieval settlement studies during the previous three decades; they were concerned primarily with sites which were represented by earthwork remains, and particularly with sites which had been villages or hamlets. The MCD categories of 'Deserted Medieval Village', and 'Shrunken Medieval Village' were drawn from the authoritative texts (eg Beresford and Hurst 1971, 19–20, 304–5).

Fortuitously, the emergence of the MCDs coincided with a rapidly growing consensus among medieval settlement researchers that the thirty-year focus on medieval villages gave an inadequate perspective on settlement studies. The neglect of dispersed forms of settlement, other than those surrounded by moats (Aberg 1978), was attacked most directly by David Austin (Aston 1989, 233, 245–6), though the amalgamation of the Medieval Village Research Group (MVRG) and the Moated Sites Research Group in 1986, and their reconstitution as the Medieval Settlement Research Group, had already signified the willingness of the research community to pay due regard to dispersed settlement studies. The MVRG's papers on dispersed settlement (Fox *et al* 1983) first placed such issues firmly on the research agenda; Peter Christopher Warner's study of greenside settlement in Suffolk, published in 1987, and Christopher Dyer's work in the West Midlands, on the dispersed settlements of Pendock (1990) and Hanbury (1991), represented significant advances in the detailed study of regions where, in the Middle Ages, nucleated settlements were sparse. The review of the medieval settlement MCDs therefore provided an opportunity to incorporate these shifts in research focus. The two MCDs for deserted and shrunken (or shifted) villages were abandoned, and replaced by new documents: one dealing with 'Medieval (nucleated) Villages', the other with 'Dispersed Medieval Settlements'.

The growing interest in dispersed settlement forms during the 1980s can be linked to an increasing emphasis on what is called 'landscape history'. The first issue of a journal bearing that title, which appeared in 1979, contained several contributions from staff of the West Yorkshire Archaeology Unit, an organisation which had recently carried out a comprehensive study of medieval settlement throughout that county. Though West Yorkshire is located largely in what we will define as the 'Central Province' – dominated by nucleations – it retained throughout medieval and post-medieval times much of its 'dispersed' character, particularly in the west. The township of *Northowram*, near Halifax, for example contained within its 3,400 acres more than thirty dispersed settlements in the thirteenth and fourteenth centuries. Some were probably single farmsteads; others, such as *Horlawegrenehouses* and *Cliffehouses*, were evidently hamlets (Faull and Moorhouse 1981, 603-6). In other parts of the Central Province the traditional unit of settlement research was the village site, its study boundary substantially defined by the perimeter where the earthworks of tofts, crofts and back lanes meet the ridge and furrow of the former open fields. However, regions like West Yorkshire, dominated by dispersed habitations, require a broader context of study. One need only glance at the published plan of dispersed settlement earthworks at Shenley Brook End, Buckinghamshire (Everson 1995, fig 87), to realise the futility in such cases of attempting to extract habitation sites from associated tangles of arable fields, common pastures and trackways.

The decision to tackle dispersed settlement regions in full in MPP led inevitably, therefore, to attempts to characterise those regions on a broader basis, assessing the density of dispersed elements, and the extent to which they were intercalated with nucleations – in effect assessing their *definitive characteristics*. The descriptive process could then be extended to include types of enclosures, field systems, road networks, associated industrial activity and other 'landscape' features – *associated characteristics* – which can be set against the background of the new terrain map appearing in this Atlas (Figs 14, 16, and 18). Such regional characterisation allows all aspects of settlement, both medieval and post-medieval, archaeological remains and functioning entities, to be placed within an appropriate context. Without it, the relatively unspectacular remains in counties such as Cheshire and Suffolk would be considerably undervalued by comparison with the far more impressive earthworks of abandoned upland farms in areas such as Dartmoor, Cornwall and the Lake District. Indeed, even within those parts of the country which had been dominated in medieval times by nucleated settlement, the ability to assess well-known deserted villages within their regional context provided an opportunity to give serious consideration to sites which might otherwise have been dismissed as having relatively poor and indistinct earthworks, sites which might, nevertheless, prove to be of crucial importance for understanding the settlement history of that region. However, before the idea of the region can be used as an effective tool of management and research some national perspective should be available, providing definition of the contrasts present and then presenting them in a usable map. Thus Figure 1, a complete mosaic of local regions, has been established using the evidence of the two national maps of nucleated and dispersed settlement (Figs 9, 10 and 13). These regions represent the lowest rung of a hierarchy extending upwards though sub-provinces to three main settlement provinces. While subsequent work may well modify the details of many local regions, the three provinces represent a stable framework for long-term future use.

The mosaic of regions must be assessed against four frameworks: the units of local administration, the ancient, traditional counties, the National Grid, and finally, all of the other historical distributions within this study. Figures 1 and 2 present the regions, the historic counties and units of local government at a scale of 1:2 million to allow direct comparison with Figure 3, showing rural settlement. Figure 2 is the result of a series of compromises, for the decades since 1970 have seen numerous adjustments in the pattern of county boundaries are designed to allow a user to locate any area of interest as easily and quickly as possible. Local administration units are often the framework for archaeological sites and monuments records. The ancient counties retain their importance as the framework for archive materials. The National Grid, structured around squares with sides 100 by 100 kilometres, further subdivided into squares 10 by 10 kilometres, is capable of even finer division, down to the level of the individual metre square or even beyond (Harley 1975, 24–9). More obviously a pure measure of space than the more fluent

county lines, both are nevertheless reminders of James Corner's words that 'Measures facilitate possession. They enable one to occupy, control and manipulate land' (Corner and MacLean 1996, 69). It will be seen at once that neither the ancient nor the modern units of local administration coincide with the settlement regions which have been mapped. This is an important point to note, for it has implications for the structure of both historical sources and archaeological records. Any administrative unit or traditional county will contain parts of several settlement regions, which will themselves extend into other, adjacent counties. In order to grasp fully the character of these regions it is necessary to free one's perspective from England's administrative framework. This demand will sharpen rather than blur understanding of national rural settlement diversity. Figure 1, the mosaic of regions we have created, must be explained and justified in the pages which follow. The terms and notations for the provinces, sub-provinces and local regions which are used in the following pages are listed in the Appendix.

Landscapes and regions

Countrysides of the present contain complex mixtures of elements, some of which are natural, some of which are artefacts bequeathed by former generations, entities which are now often substantively divorced from their original setting. At any point in time past any given countryside would comprise mixtures of elements inherited from both the immediate past and from even earlier antecedents. Processes of creation, decay, adaptation, renewal, sometimes in the context of dramatic transformations over long or short periods of time, generate what the historian F W Maitland termed 'that complex palimpsest' (Maitland 1897; 1960 reprint, 38), bearing comparison with an overwritten document. This creates tensions, for the landscape is a resource, from which contemporary society must, in part, obtain a living, but it is also a source for all concerned with the past. In M R G Conzen's words settlement is the 'geographical record of its own evolution' (Conzen in Isaac and Allan 1949, 76).

The use of the word landscape to describe this complex palimpsest is a matter which needs some consideration. Although most ideas have multiple roots, for English readers the concept of the cultural landscape was closely defined in a classic paper by Carl Sauer entitled *The Morphology of Landscape* (Leighley, 1963, 315–50). In this study Sauer reviewed what had been and in 1938 was still the object of geographical study, showing that the German roots of the term *Landschaft* imply the study of 'the content of areas', both of the entities present and the connections between these: he argued that human activities act upon both unaltered and altered nature to generate cultural landscapes, places and areas, whose distinctive and unique associations of elements (by definition location is always unique) are worthy of study, analysis, comparison and explanation. The time dimension can never be excluded, although the duration taken into account may vary from a few decades to several thousand years.

The word landscape was originally introduced into English from the Netherlands as a painter's term, with all that this implies in terms of perceptions, judgements and values; indeed Sauer comments on this link (Leighley 1963, 322). In philological terms landscape uses two Old English words – 'land' and 'scape' – to integrate two ideas, the first implying 'a tract of land', with the second meaning 'create', 'ordain' or 'appoint', as seen in craftsmanship and workmanship, where individuals and artefacts are involved. The collective may also be implied as in township – the territory of a -*tun*, or local farming community. Common usage such as that seen in W G Hoskins' *The Making of the English Landscape* (originally published in 1955, but revised in 1976: see Taylor in Hoskins 1988) supports the general use of the term to designate the components of the artefactual scene which, in close combination with wholly natural elements, give distinctive character to tracts of countryside, perhaps even including and embracing townscapes. This usage has the sanction of scholarship (Beresford and St Joseph 1958: 1979, 3; Aston and Rowley 1974, 21–7; Cantor 1982, 17–23; Everitt 1986, 1–13; Taylor in Hoskins 1988, 7–9). Of course, such a definition in no way excludes artistic or perceptual approaches. No narrow limits need be sought or accepted (Selman 1994, *passim*).

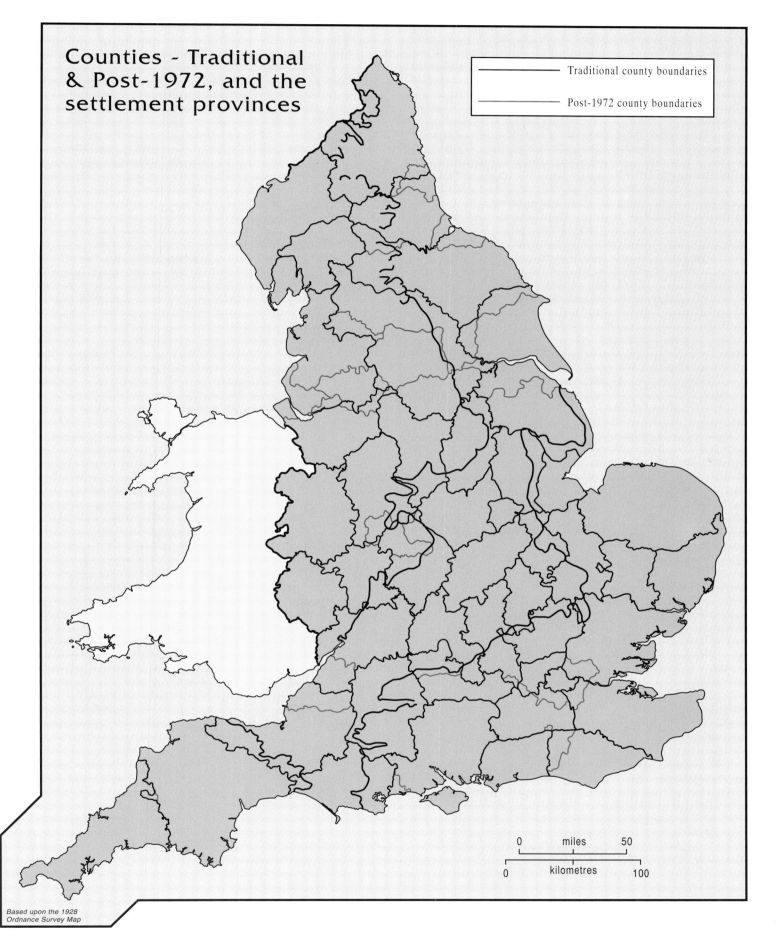

Counties - Traditional & Post-1972, and the settlement provinces

Traditional county boundaries

Post-1972 county boundaries

0   miles   50

0   kilometres   100

Based upon the 1928
Ordnance Survey Map

Figure 2

A second term which is also charged with many possible meanings is the word 'region'. There is no simple, single definition, although the common view is of an area made distinctive because it is characterised by distinctive features, normally a particular combination of physical and/or cultural entities, what may be called landscape elements. Many shades of definition are possible: regions can be pragmatically defined in terms of one or more dominant features, for example a particular type of settlement or land-use, or by physical features such as gravel lands or chalkland, or as the area dominated by a particular type of economic system. Such simple cases emphasise both the contrast between formal regions, characterised by the presence of defined distinctive elements, and functional regions, defined quite simply by elements of function, and the presence of both natural elements, given by nature, and cultural elements or artefacts, created by human technology. On the other hand, regional definition can draw upon subtleties such as life-styles and involve the perceptions of both the inhabitants and/or neighbours. E Estyn Evans touched a vital point when he noted in 1973 that Sauer's use of the term 'geographical personality' embraced 'the whole dynamic relation of life and land' (1992, 68). In fact the roots of this holistic idea, often defined by using the term 'personality', are deeply rooted and are best exemplified by the French term *pays*, implying an area possessing its own innate identity (Braudel 1989, 37, 41–57; Everitt 1986, 5–6, 43–68).

The use of the term 'geographical personality' recalls inevitably Sir Cyril Fox, and his exploration of the meaning of archaeological distributions in Britain through the concept of Highland and Lowland Zones, defined on the basis of geological characteristics (Fox 1952, 28–32). The Highland and Lowland Zones together form a model of regional contrasts devised in 1902 by Sir Halford Mackinder; they were created then and not (*pace* Fowler 1978, 2) 'by the land-use history of the preceding 3,000 years'. Fox used the model as a background for the spatial distribution of archaeological artefacts in much the same way that the settlement provinces have been used here. Furthermore, parts of the Highland/Lowland boundary coincide with stretches of the boundary between the Central Province and Northern and Western Province (Fox 1952, map B). There are, however, considerable areas of disagreement, and there is, of course, no South-eastern Province in Fox's study. Fox used what he termed 'the natural boundary': this Atlas employs cultural data informed by contrasts in terrain. This is not the place to undertake detailed comparative analysis, but one point should be made. The effect of the Highland/Lowland model is to conflate our Central and South-eastern Provinces and thereby to obscure a number of marked regional contrasts. Thus Peter Fowler has characterised the Lowland Zone as one of nucleated settlement, with dispersed settlement characterising the Highland Zone (Fowler in Limbery and Evans 1978, 7). Such a contrast is entirely acceptable within the terms of the Mackinder/Fox model. Here it is simply argued that the three provinces model offers much greater scope for the sophisticated analysis of regional settlement contrasts in England.

A further model of both national and local regions, forming a complete and articulated national mosaic, was constructed by Sir Dudley Stamp as part of the Land Utilisation Survey conducted between 1930 and 1947 (Stamp 1962). This, created at a time when there was a slump in agriculture, was undoubtedly a foundation study, and the fine series of volumes – often incorporating an historical perspective involving the use of eighteenth- and nineteenth-century maps to establish a broad picture of earlier land-use – now represents an important historical record in its own right. In this present study relatively slight use has been made of Stamp's work, a curious tribute because his synthesis was so complete, so thorough and so soundly based that it was necessary to be independent, to avoid the criticism of creating an anachronistic view of earlier circumstances.

Further important national views appear in the work of Joan Thirsk. Two volumes of *The Cambridge Agrarian History of England* (volumes IV and V: Thirsk 1987) have included substantial analyses of regional contrasts in farming in both the seventeenth and eighteenth centuries. These are important maps, lying between the Land Utilisation Survey and *Domesday Book*; they were constructed by using data from contemporary sources, plotted on Ordnance Survey 1:125,000 'administrative' maps and then carefully defining local boundaries. While the local regions identified are in detail complex, they can be subsumed within a framework of three fundamental farming types: wood pasture, open pasture and mixed types, the last being heavily orientated towards arable grain production within townfields. The third national survey to parallel this work by Stamp and Thirsk is that by Sir Clifford Darby and his co-workers in their magisterial reconstruction of the geography of England revealed by *Domesday Book* of 1086. Darby produced a national synthesis, a remarkable, indeed unique view of a country in the final quarter of the eleventh century. Unfortunately, because each administrative county was treated as a serparate entity by the individual scholar who shaped the Domesday maps, the local regions which they identified are impossible to synthesise into a complete national picture.

Maps and landscapes

There is a fundamental question we cannot ignore: 'What is the relationship between the map and the landscape?' (Turnbull 1989, *passim*). Any map is a representation of a territory or a piece of territory – one form of model. The adoption of a wholly vertical view separates a map from a picture, and selection of what is to be included or excluded is crucial in all map-making. So it is that maps reflect more than physical facts: they reflect the states of mind of those who create and read them. Furthermore, the nature, availability and character of the source materials also provides a crucial filter, affecting what can be selected by the map-maker. No matter how ingenious the cartographer, maps can show only limited elements of the environment, the life-styles operating, or the factors affecting the inhabitants. A map may represent an 'indexical' statement, two-dimensional, descriptive and specific, or it may be non-indexical, analytical, generalised, abstracted and of more general application, touching the imagination as much as factual statements of location, quality, quantity and direction.

Bringing together landscapes and maps activates more complex issues: a single map comprises not one but many layers, some being artefacts of construction, while others relate to and reflect genetic layers present within the real landscapes of which the maps are representations. It will be useful to attempt to define these, and it appears helpful to identify, initially at least, five broad categories:

a) the immediate surface layers, involving a complex network of material activity which is the product of the immediate past. These are essentially soft forms, which result from cultivation, cropping, grazing and even moving and resting, windblow, variations in soil moisture and soil movement, in vegetation status – from dormancy to full florescence and decay – broadly, in fact, all daily, weekly and seasonal activities and processes. In archaeological terms these are surprisingly important, for they can be preserved by chance and their immediacy has much to tell us about everyday usages; in character they can range from plough marks, evidence for annual activity, to deposits of vegetation recording the character of one season.

b) functionally defined structures, including hard surfaces such as roads and buildings, but also extending to the linear and spatial components of the mosaic of yards, tracks, open spaces, arable fields, woodlands, pastures and enclosures; in them is vast diversity of composition, structure, colour and texture seen at local, regional and national scales. At any one time their existence frames the artefactual landscapes within which work, leisure and beliefs are pursued, in which natural and cultural elements are integrated, while their hard structures ensure that some at least are passed from one generation to another, and so possess significant durations in time.

c) a functionally important but seemingly invisible network intruded between layers (a) and (b) consisting of proprietary systems, rights of ownership and usage. These divide the physical land and the artefacts upon and within it into a tightly tessellated mosaic of proprietary land units, each cell representing a decision-making entity which is crucial for all decisions about land use, be this a building, yard space, minute garden or plot, close or open field strip, or vast grazing tract (Denman and Prodano 1972, 11–35). Once again, although these do change, they are certainly not ephemeral, but possess definite duration in time, so that tenurial conditions having roots one hundred, five hundred or over a thousand years earlier are invisibly present in today's landscapes and townscapes. This is evident in Figure 22 where the landownership patterns within which village depopulation appeared had effects which are manifest some four hundred years later. Landownership and tenure can be subtly visible in the landscape, in the quality of boundary and gate maintenance, in distinctive building styles or colours, the hues of the fields, reflecting management and manuring practices, and more dramatically in the presence of walled parklands and woodlands: they are also defined within the documentary record.

d) those elements which derive from the existence or absence of belief and ritual, fashion and iconoclasm, expedience and the imponderable attitudes of mind, all of which have effects upon landscapes from the dramatic to the subtle. The creation of sacred enclosures, of special areas for leisure purposes, of parks and gardens, of National Parks, are all ways of delimiting special landscapes and reaching for something beyond the agrarian routine.

e) finally, beneath and within elements (b), (c) and (d), elements of antecedent landscapes; some of these are no more than mere fragments, but others comprise visible structures, buildings or their sites, linear boundaries and substantive areas. Visible or ephemerally visible, functional or relict, these extend across the full spectrum from inhabited, used buildings, to functioning parts of the present landscape, ancient banks, waterways or routes, to mere shapes, shadows and colours, briefly and discontinuously visible as the day, the seasons and the years pulse. Nevertheless, these elements are historically and archaeologically important, for they are definable portions of past landscapes which can be seen, preserved and/or researched – tangible raw materials of investigation and scholarship.

These elements making up the rural scene, and here artificially dissected (Figs 21 and 29), are more than mere artefactual or archival survivals: the landscape in all its aspects is structured by people to give expression to social relations, and reciprocally to frame social relations. A key element in structuring is to give access to and control of space, and the components of differentiated space. In the words of James Corner:

> ... the way a landscape looks is considered inseparable from, and integral to, the day-to-day activities and values of its occupants. In this way quality and value cannot be detached from quantity, just as spacings, tolerances, and limits cannot be considered separately from ideology, ethics and social responsibility. Thus, the measures of land have a threefold nature: they are at once the guide, the outcome, and the gauge of cultural activity.
>
> (Corner and MacLean 1996, xviii–xix)

Corner argues that

> ... to continue to relate to the land either as an exploitable resource or as merely a scenic phenomenon is to fail to recognise the dynamic and interactive connectivity between human life and the natural environment.
>
> (ibid xix)

and this is fundamental to the perception offered here.

Thus a common townfield is as much a social construction as is a park or land with right of free warren. In this view even the uses of the landscape for 'ritual' purposes are included, through which the impact of sacred activity on the land can become a representation of human relations with nature, gods, and the universe.

Faced with this complexity, three categories of question should be isolated:

(1) What is being mapped? What are the strengths and limitations of the map?

(2) Which levels do the maps represent? Can they provide information about significant variations in the character of past cultural landscapes or are they merely recycling unsuitable and generalised representations of long-established cultural responses to the physical enivironment, ie the Highland/Lowland contrast in disguise?

(3) What 'realities' do the maps construct? Would the contrasts which have been detected have been meaningful in terms of the lifestyles of past times? Can we use what can be mapped as surrogates or substitutes for things which cannot be mapped?

There are no easy or short answers to any of these questions, but at their simplest level these maps provide synoptic images which are designed to frame observations, descriptions, questions, analyses and explanations. To do this, particular bodies of source material must be assembled. Pragmatically, all maps are bounded by the coastline and the arbitrary but historically durable boundaries of Wales and Scotland, and all measured by the invisible presence of the cadastral structure of the National Grid. Nevertheless, and to pre-empt later arguments, we believe that the images which have been filtered out have developed as a product of human/land interactions within a deep matrix of time. We believe that within our primary settlement maps, ie those derived from a close analysis of nineteenth-century sources, are latent images of far earlier patterns, present but deeply concealed and camouflaged by the background noise of the detail which results from the compression of evidence from many periods into the one plane. For this reason we include in Figures 21–6 a reminder of the time spans involved, in the form of a vertical bar-scale.

4 The national maps

The maps are presented at three scales. The working drawings were originally made at a scale of 1:250,000, a quarter inch to one mile, which were then reduced and translated into the computer using a basic outline framework derived from an Ordnance Survey 1:1 million topographic map of 1928, to which were added the National Grid and the outlines of county boundaries. All of the important maps appear in this Atlas in a full page format, while those of settlement and terrain have been enlarged to produce three sectional maps for closer study. In contrast, some of the supporting maps are reproduced at a smaller scale. All maps represent a compromise between the scale of the base map, the data to be depicted and the nature of the graphics used.

It is a paradox that at the time of writing the larger scale maps have not yet been fully used; of course, as the text of this Atlas shows, the distributions have been evaluated, described, compared and questioned, indeed all of the other figures included are part of this process. Nevertheless, there has been no attempt as yet, for example, to describe the distribution of settlement in relation to the varied terrains, and not entirely through fear of this exercise being described as 'neo-deterministic': there are clear and unambiguous relationships, wholly familiar to most readers and users of this Atlas. A primary objective here is to furnish maps which can be used by others to establish contexts for the study and assessment of individual sites. A more thorough analysis of the data which have been generated must await a study which is still in preparation.

At this point we must assess some of the inherent qualities of the settlement maps, the manner in which they present data, and the implications of variations in scales. Figure 10 is a type of distribution which may best be described as 'specific', and although each dot is not to a definite scale, each has a precise meaning. This reveals the fine detail of the national distribution, and were the map to be enlarged from the present scale of reproduction it would retain much of its integrity and value. It is even possible to enlarge it sufficiently to create county and regional scale maps such as are seen in Figures 19 and 20.

Furthermore, so far as was possible Figure 10 records 100% of the distribution, and we know this because of the nature of the source and the mapping procedure. Many archaeological maps, using dots to demonstrate the presence of particular features, are inevitably more partial and this makes them difficult to interpret. In some cases the mapped distribution is sufficiently complete – 90%, 77%, or 53% – for the substance and at least some of the detail of the distribution to be ascertained: moated sites and deserted villages undoubtedly fall into this category, but with many archaeological distributions it is rare to be able to determine with any real precision what proportion of the whole has actually been recorded and mapped.

In sharp contrast, Figure 9 records a 'generalised' distribution, one that is essentially 'out of focus' in comparison with Figure 10. As noted earlier, the mapping system has been devised to avoid the excessive detail which would be generated if all aspects of dispersion were mapped. Thus, while Figure 10 can be enlarged, in Figure 9 the degree of generalisation is too great to allow meaningful enlargement much beyond the scale of a single county.

Comparative material presents a particular problem: because maps drawn to other scales and on other bases rarely fit the standard exemplar precisely, they have to be slightly transformed to get the best fit. This involves stretching and/or shrinking, sometimes uniformly, sometimes differentially, so that a small degree of distortion is inevitable. In practical terms all permit firm generalisations to be made at the national scale, at the scale of the administrative county, and even allow the subtleties of finer detail to be explored.

In conclusion, it should be emphasised that while the settlement and terrain maps are as accurate as we can make them, there are limitations deriving from the heterogeneous ways in which the diverse materials have been assembled. In short, as an examination of Figure 10 will show, it is perfectly feasible to envisage a 10 by 10 kilometre square on all the national maps of this series, but some uncertainties must exist about the placing of symbols within that area. When using the settlement maps, tests suggest that they are often, perhaps even normally, usable at a large scale, but that the evidence becomes less reliable when the same exercise is attempted with, for example, the distribution map of deserted villages (Fig 21) because irrespective of the accuracy of the original plot, the distribution has been brought to the present page through the filter of many photographings, reductions and enlargements. Errors of commission and omission there must be, but these should not detract from the cartographic vision presented in this Atlas.

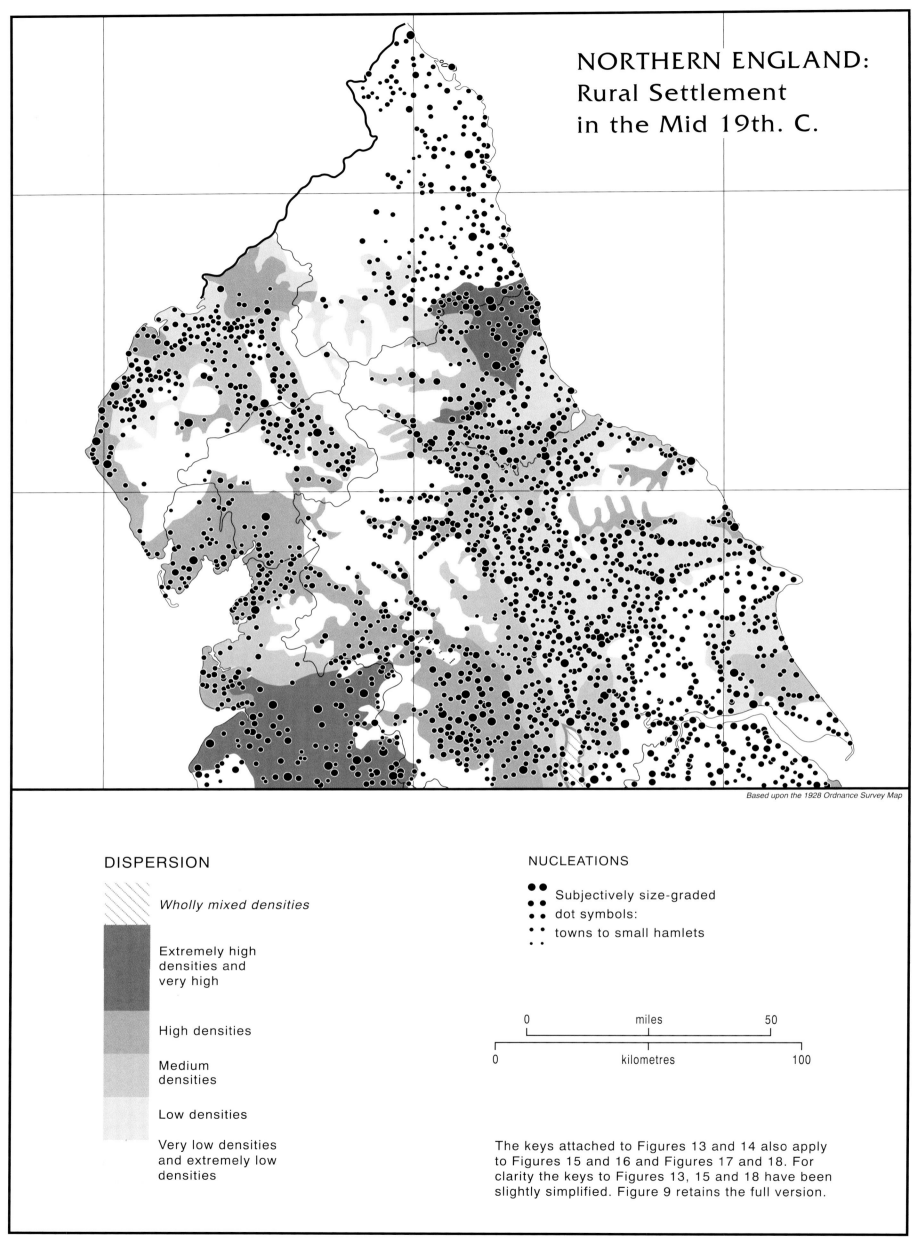

NORTHERN ENGLAND:
Rural Settlement
in the Mid 19th. C.

Based upon the 1928 Ordnance Survey Map

DISPERSION

Wholly mixed densities

Extremely high
densities and
very high

High densities

Medium
densities

Low densities

Very low densities
and extremely low
densities

NUCLEATIONS

Subjectively size-graded
dot symbols:
towns to small hamlets

0   miles   50

0   kilometres   100

The keys attached to Figures 13 and 14 also apply
to Figures 15 and 16 and Figures 17 and 18. For
clarity the keys to Figures 13, 15 and 18 have been
slightly simplified. Figure 9 retains the full version.

Figure 13

©*BKR / SW / EH*

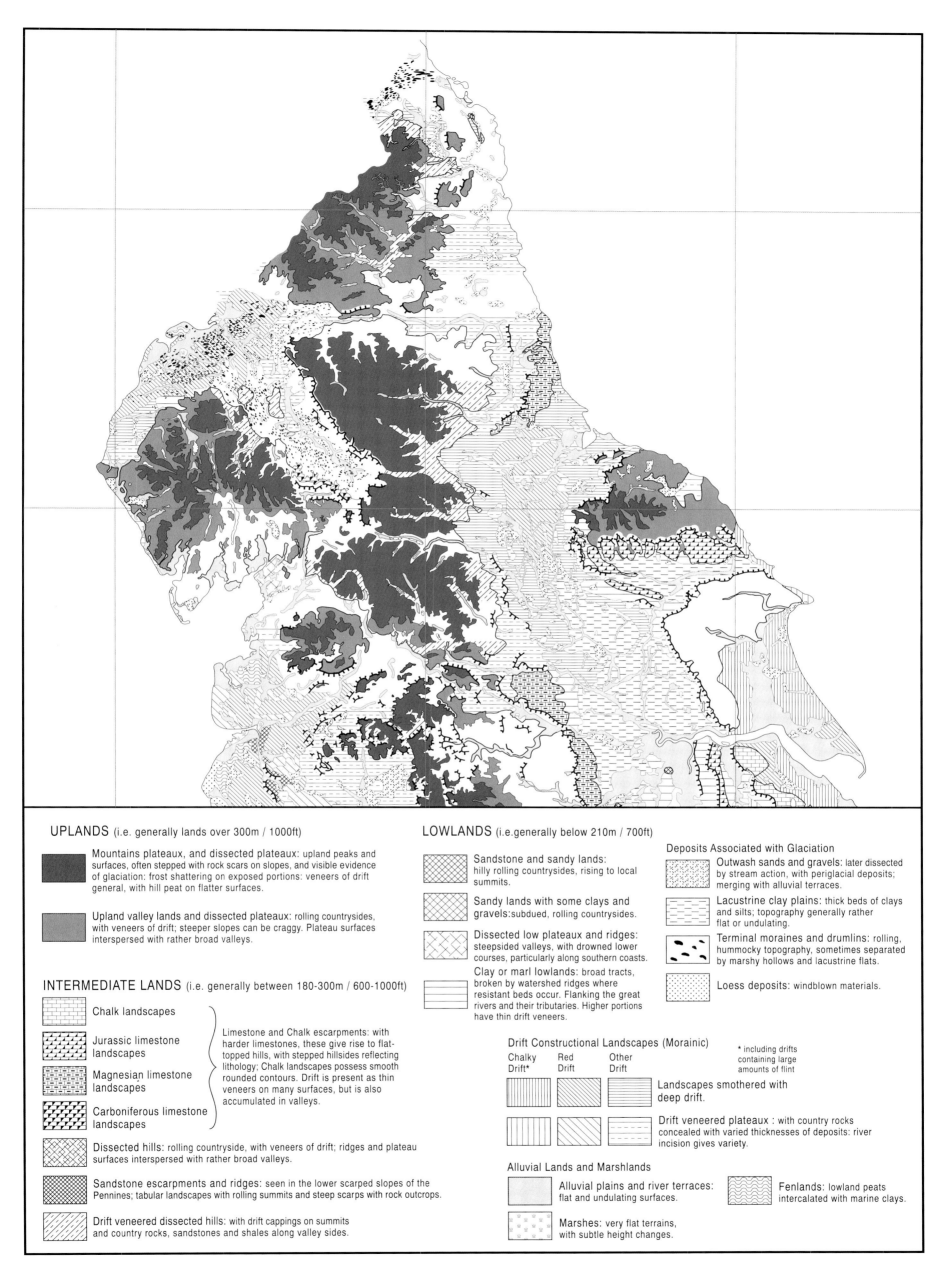

UPLANDS (i.e. generally lands over 300m / 1000ft)

Mountains plateaux, and dissected plateaux: upland peaks and surfaces, often stepped with rock scars on slopes, and visible evidence of glaciation: frost shattering on exposed portions: veneers of drift general, with hill peat on flatter surfaces.

Upland valley lands and dissected plateaux: rolling countrysides, with veneers of drift; steeper slopes can be craggy. Plateau surfaces interspersed with rather broad valleys.

INTERMEDIATE LANDS (i.e. generally between 180-300m / 600-1000ft)

Chalk landscapes

Jurassic limestone landscapes

Magnesian limestone landscapes

Carboniferous limestone landscapes

Limestone and Chalk escarpments: with harder limestones, these give rise to flat-topped hills, with stepped hillsides reflecting lithology; Chalk landscapes possess smooth rounded contours. Drift is present as thin veneers on many surfaces, but is also accumulated in valleys.

Dissected hills: rolling countryside, with veneers of drift; ridges and plateau surfaces interspersed with rather broad valleys.

Sandstone escarpments and ridges: seen in the lower scarped slopes of the Pennines; tabular landscapes with rolling summits and steep scarps with rock outcrops.

Drift veneered dissected hills: with drift cappings on summits and country rocks, sandstones and shales along valley sides.

LOWLANDS (i.e.generally below 210m / 700ft)

Sandstone and sandy lands: hilly rolling countrysides, rising to local summits.

Sandy lands with some clays and gravels:subdued, rolling countrysides.

Dissected low plateaux and ridges: steepsided valleys, with drowned lower courses, particularly along southern coasts.

Clay or marl lowlands: broad tracts, broken by watershed ridges where resistant beds occur. Flanking the great rivers and their tributaries. Higher portions have thin drift veneers.

Deposits Associated with Glaciation

Outwash sands and gravels: later dissected by stream action, with periglacial deposits; merging with alluvial terraces.

Lacustrine clay plains: thick beds of clays and silts; topography generally rather flat or undulating.

Terminal moraines and drumlins: rolling, hummocky topography, sometimes separated by marshy hollows and lacustrine flats.

Loess deposits: windblown materials.

Drift Constructional Landscapes (Morainic)

Chalky Drift*	Red Drift	Other Drift	

* including drifts containing large amounts of flint

Landscapes smothered with deep drift.

Drift veneered plateaux : with country rocks concealed with varied thicknesses of deposits: river incision gives variety.

Alluvial Lands and Marshlands

Alluvial plains and river terraces: flat and undulating surfaces.

Fenlands: lowland peats intercalated with marine clays.

Marshes: very flat terrains, with subtle height changes.

Figure 14

21

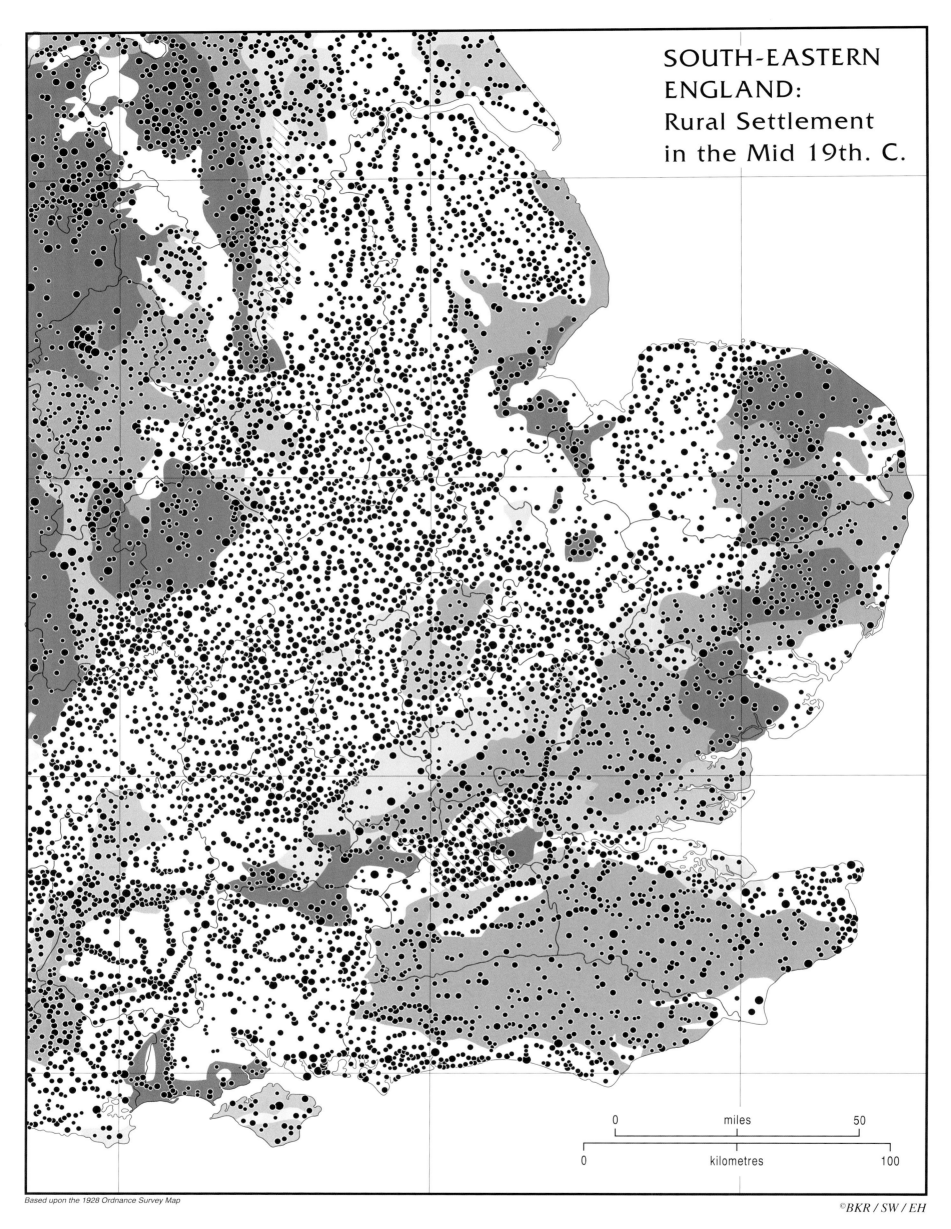

SOUTH-EASTERN
ENGLAND:
Rural Settlement
in the Mid 19th. C.

0   miles   50

0   kilometres   100

Based upon the 1928 Ordnance Survey Map

©BKR / SW / EH

Figure 15

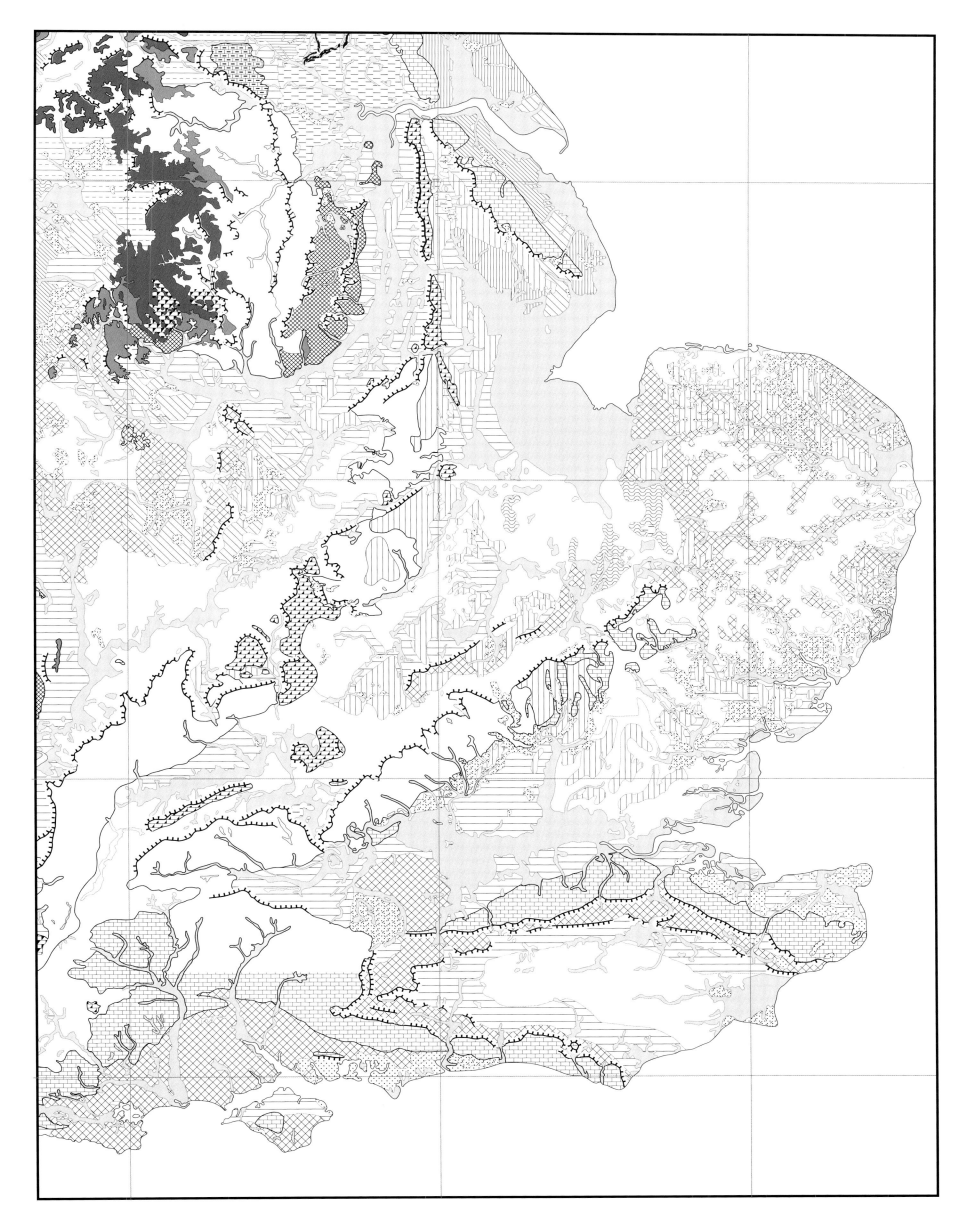

Figure 16

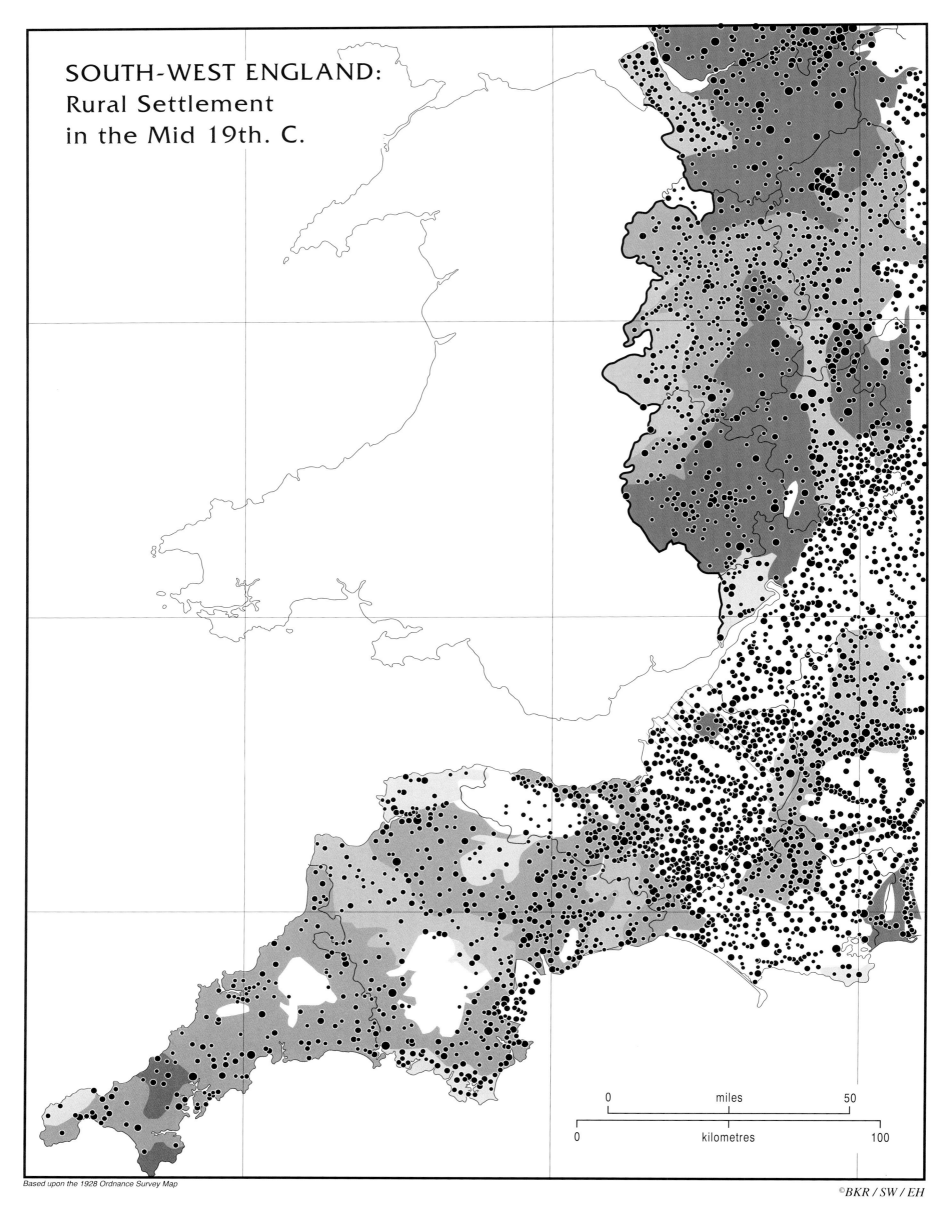

SOUTH-WEST ENGLAND:
Rural Settlement
in the Mid 19th. C.

0 miles 50

0 kilometres 100

Based upon the 1928 Ordnance Survey Map

©BKR / SW / EH

Figure 17

Figure 18

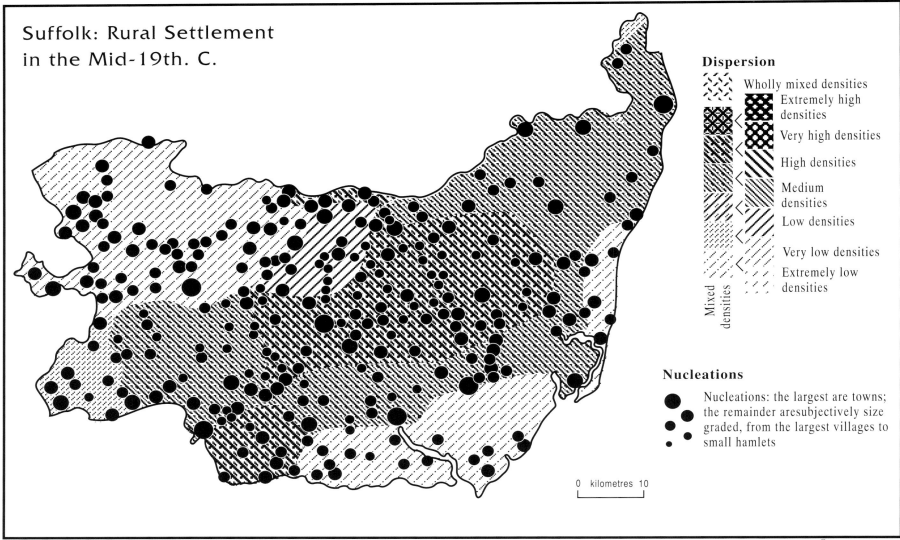

Suffolk: Rural Settlement
in the Mid-19th. C.

Dispersion

Wholly mixed densities
Extremely high densities
Very high densities
High densities
Medium densities
Low densities
Very low densities
Extremely low densities

Mixed densities

Nucleations

Nucleations: the largest are towns;
the remainder are subjectively size
graded, from the largest villages to
small hamlets

0   kilometres   10

©1996 EH/ BKR & SW

Figure 19

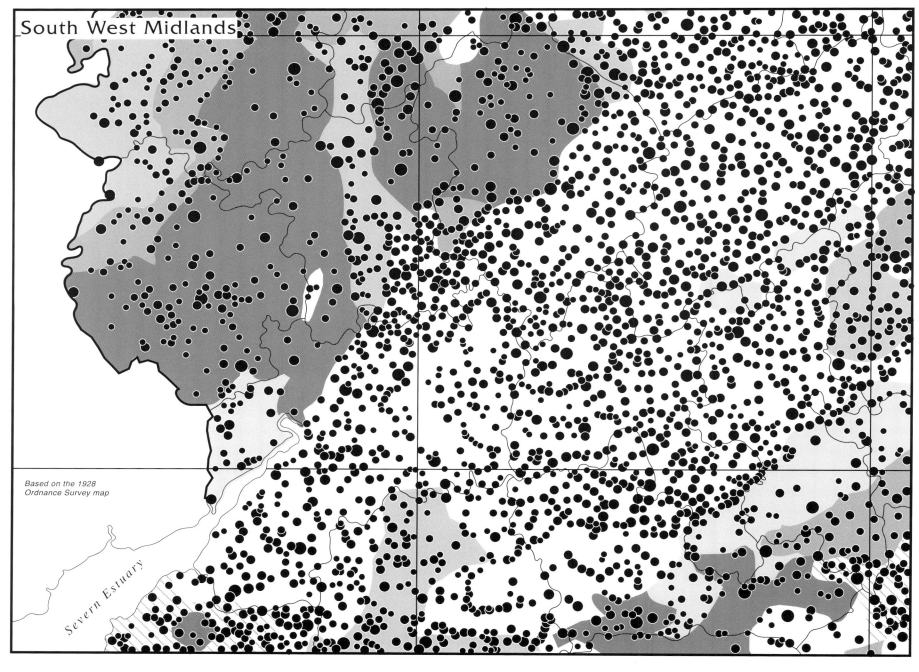

South West Midlands

Based on the 1928
Ordnance Survey map

Severn Estuary

Figure 20

5 Perspectives in time

Throughout this Atlas, the maps of mid-nineteenth century settlement are intended as an analytical tool, to be used with other national distributions to disentangle and understand the palimpsest of regional variation and to provide a broad chronological measure for the generation of characteristics which led ultimately to the nineteenth-century pattern. The starting point, the most directly comparable distribution (Fig 21), is that of deserted medieval villages as recorded up to 1968 (Beresford and Hurst 1971, fig 13). On one level the broad correlation between the distribution of deserted villages and the distribution of nucleated settlements still extant in the nineteenth century is unremarkable. Yet the general thinning of nucleated settlements – rather than the total extinction of villages in certain parts of the country, and their complete immunity from depopulation in other regions – is itself a matter of research interest. Further, the distributions are not wholly coincident. There is, for example, a marked lack of deserted medieval villages recorded in most of the CPNSL sub-province of the Central Province (Fig 1). Was there no depopulation of medieval villages here; were there depopulations which have failed systematically to achieve record in the antiquarian and archaeological literature; or is this an area which lacked nucleated settlements in quantity until post-medieval times? While in an earlier discussion we made an eastward adjustment of the Central Province boundary on the basis of likely alterations in the overall settlement pattern by industrialisation, careful study of Figures 21–6 and Figure 29 suggests that this point undoubtedly needs closer, more detailed attention than can be given here. Nevertheless, on the grounds of other national distributions, especially woodland, we hypothesise that this area was assimilated into the Central Province of nucleations only in post-medieval times. A second example shows the contrary problem: the density of deserted villages recorded in Norfolk was not fully predicted from the pattern of nucleation/dispersion densities in the nineteenth century. Was village depopulation a much more comprehensive phenomenon here; or should we look more closely at the types of settlement (especially the ribbons of homesteads along the edges of commons and greens) which have been described as villages? These issues have been explored in greater depth elsewhere (Wrathmell 1994, 182–4).

The next example concerns population rather than settlements, and draws upon the work of John Dewdney who has created for us a parish-by-parish plot of the 1851 census data, a task not undertaken before (Fig 22). Selecting the parishes which, in the 1851 census, were recorded as containing the lowest quartile of the total distribution of the population, there is broad correlation to be found between those regions which provide records of medieval village depopulation and those 'lowland' parishes which in 1851 were sparsely inhabited. This may seem to tell us only what could have been expected, until one remembers that in many parts of the Central Province the bulk of depopulations took place before the seventeenth century, and what we are seeing is the residual impact of the socio-economic changes which led to village depopulation, still evident in the English countryside some two, three or even four centuries later – and this despite the rapid changes caused by the Industrial Revolution.

Indeed, it is such long-term trends which can be examined most easily at the national level, as in the case of the next map in this section, showing the enclosure of open townfields by Act of Parliament (Fig 23). Few would deny a general association between nucleated settlements and large, open townfields, and such an association is graphically supported at a national scale by the coincident patterns of deserted medieval villages, the nucleated settlements of the mid-nineteenth-century Central Province and open townfields affected by Parliamentary enclosure (Slater 1907, 73). Yet there are, once again, interesting disparities, the most obvious being in north-east England, with its lack of Parliamentary townfield enclosure inside the Central Province, and in the western half of Norfolk, with its heavy density of enclosure records outside that Province. We would argue that north-east England differed considerably from the Midland zones, in terms of both its tenurial conditions and its agrarian circumstances: its open townfields, for example, never swamped the areas of permanent pasture as they did in some parts of the East Midlands (Hodgson in Harley and Baker 1973, 145). These differences encouraged early enclosure, either by manorial fiat or by private agreement among the freeholders, as can be seen in the recorded townfield enclosures in the southern part of Northumberland (Wrathmell 1975, 275–81). The anomalous enclosure records for western Norfolk have been discussed by Homans (1969, 19–21). There is not space here to consider such regional disparities in detail; suffice it to say that the contradiction in these maps can generate debate just as much as the coincidences.

Oliver Rackham, whose *History of the English Countryside* (1986) contains an important seminal map, has argued that England can be divided into three sections: a central one, comprising 'planned countryside', framed by two others, both, in his words, 'ancient countryside'. The former he characterised as 'the Cambridgeshire type', ... the England of big villages, few busy roads, thin hawthorn hedges, windswept brick farms, and ivied clumps of trees in the corners of fields: a predictable land of wide views, sweeping sameness, and straight lines'. The two latter he designated the Essex or Hertfordshire type, 'the England of hamlets, medieval farms in hollows of the hills, lonely moats and great barns in the clay lands, pollards and ancient trees, cavernous holloways and many footpaths, fords, irregularly-shaped groves with thick hedges colourful with maple, dogwood and spindle – an intricate land of mystery and surprise' (Rackham 1986, 4–5). This model presages our three provinces, though it has been constructed from entirely different data.

Figure 24 takes another step: it integrates within a single map the varied county distributions of woodland reconstructed by Darby and his co-workers, simplifying slightly, but taking advantage of the power of the computer to do what Darby was unable to do for technical reasons (Darby 1977, 64). To this have been added data derived from the technically sound but visually unimpressive map created by Rackham (1986, fig 8.7), showing the towns, villages and hamlets whose names contain Old English